W9-AEG-781

GREAT PARTY GAMES

FOR
GROWN-UPS

Phil Wiswell

Sterling Publishing Co., Inc.   New York

Library of Congress Cataloging-in-Publication Data
Wiswell, Phil.
   Great party games for grown-ups.

   Originally published under title: Great games for
grown-ups.
   Includes index.
   1. Indoor games.   2. Games.   3. Entertaining.
I. Wiswell, Phil. Great games for grown-ups.
II. Title.
GV1471.W76   1988   793   87-26717
ISBN 0-8069-6774-9 (pbk.)

Published in 1988 by Sterling Publishing Co., Inc.
Originally published in hardcover under the title, "I Hate
Charades and 49 Other New Games,"
and in paperback under the title, "Great Games for Grown-Ups"
Copyright 1981 by Sterling Publishing Co., Inc.
Two Park Avenue, New York, N.Y. 10016
Distributed in Canada by Oak Tree Press Ltd.
% Canadian Manda Group, P.O. Box 920, Station U
Toronto, Ontario, Canada M8Z 5P9
Distributed in the United Kingdom by Blandford Press
Link House, West Street, Poole, Dorset BH15 1LL, England
Distributed in Australia by Capricorn Ltd.
P.O. Box 665, Lane Cove, NSW 2066
Manufactured in the United States of America
All rights reserved

CONTENTS

INTRODUCTION

Everyone knows how to play *Charades*. Almost everyone, anyway. Consequently, *Charades* is more often
than not the only suggestion adults have when faced
with a large, active group of sophisticated players. So,
undoubtedly, the first game in this collection of the best
and newest parlor games will create a flurry of objec-
tions. I can hear readers screaming, "How can he say
he hates *Charades*? . . . *Charades* is a great game!"
True. But I get tired of playing *Charades* at every gather-
ing. Can't we play anything else?

Of course we can. You're holding the alternatives in
your hand. The games and variations presented here
come from all over the world, from all sorts of players. I
learned of a good number of them through the New
Games Foundation, a nonprofit organization dedicated
to the proposition that all people have been created
equally to "play hard, play fair, nobody hurt." Some of
these games have been my favorites for years, and have
been constantly updated with new rules and variations.
About a dozen of the games here are original, created specially for this collection. I have excluded well
known classics such as *Charades*, *Sardines*, *Murder*, and
so on because they are in every other game book in
print.

Although I hope to introduce adults to a whole new
world of play with this book, nearly all of the games are
simple enough to be played with or by children. In fact,
don't be surprised if kids beat you at a lot of these
games. Most of us have a long way to go if we ever hope

to approach games with the same enthusiasm as our children do.

I hope you experience the same pleasure I get from playing the games in this book. And, in case we end up in the same group of players sometime, I want you to suggest we play a game other than *Charades*.

Phil Wiswell

WORD
GAMES

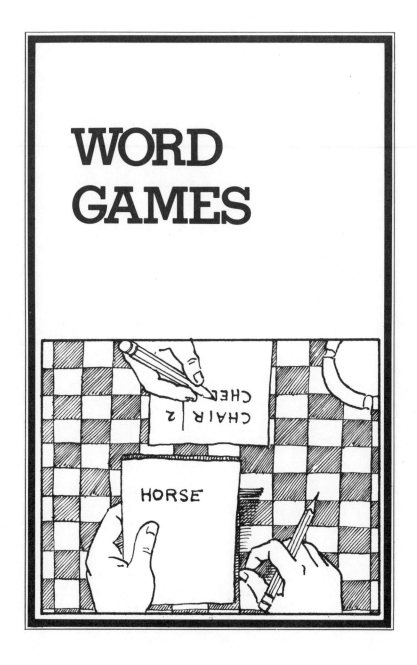

I HATE CHARADES!

Goal   To be the team that takes the least amount of time to answer the questions put to it.

Number of Players   2 teams of 3 or more players, plus a referee.

Equipment   A stopwatch, pencils, and paper.

Playing Time   About 30 minutes.

Rules of Play   This is the game for people who like the thrill of being timed, as in *Charades*, but who hate to act. I invented *I Hate Charades!* at a party. When the host announced that we were going to play *Charades*, I blurted out that we *always* play *Charades* and should try something else. "What?" everyone wanted to know. Thinking fast, I said, "I have a game called *I Hate Charades*." I was challenged for the rules. Here they are.

First, divide into two teams (or more) of equal number. Each team goes to a corner of the house to think up a list of 10 questions. These questions should have as answers a pair of rhyming words, and should contain references to both words sought. For example: What is a boring seabird? A dull gull. What do you get from the best grapes? Fine wine. What is a wonderful detail? A terrific specific . . . and so forth.

When the teams have completed their lists, they return to the playing room to begin the game. Alternately, a player from Team A and a player from Team B stands up to field a question from the other team's list. The referee uses a stopwatch to time the response and

keeps a running total for both teams. If a player cannot guess the words within one minute, the next player on his team replaces him and tries to answer, adding his time to the first player's 60 seconds. When the teams have answered all the questions, the referee adds the scores and the team with the lowest time wins.

Hint Don't make your questions too easy. You really want to stump the other team, as well as giving them a fair challenge. The longer the rhyming words you use, the harder it will be for them to guess them. Try using words like "perspiration deprivation," or "animalistic characteristic." Pairs of words need not make sense by themselves, but they must rhyme reasonably well, at least to the satisfaction of the other team.

TONTO

Goal   To describe a famous personality with a question that stumps Tonto.

Number of Players   2 or more.

Equipment   None.

Playing Time   Depending on the Tonto, 1 or 2 minutes per round.

Rules of Play   Select the first Tonto and have that person stand and face the group. The other players begin asking Tonto cryptic questions, the answers to which are the names of famous people, preceded by the word "No." For example, when asked, "Does buxom actress make good on her debts?" Tonto would answer, "No, Raquel Welch." For every question Tonto answers correctly, he receives one point. If a question seems unfair, Tonto can appeal to the mercy of the group. As soon as Tonto is stumped by a question, another Tonto takes his place—preferably the person whose question stumped him. The following examples will get you started, but you can create an infinite number of them on your own. Keep a running total of each player's score and play as many rounds as you like.

Q: Is Austrian composer giving himself up?
A: No, Joseph Haydn.

Q: Is conservative female writer uptight?
A: No, Clare Boothe Luce.

Q: Is Ogden Nash America's funniest poet?
A: No, John Greenleaf Whittier.

Q: Is powerful African leader nice guy?
A: No, Idi Amin.

Q: Is female subject of Victorian novel left out of will?
A: No, Jane Eyre.

Q: Does elderly vaudeville comedian smoke?
A: No, George Burns.

Q: Is serious half of comedy team paddling the boat?
A: No, Dan Rowan.

Q: Does Israeli Prime Minister finish?
A: No, Menachim Begin.

BOUND FOR HELL

Goal   To guess Beelzebub's secret category of words.

Number of Players   2 or more.

Equipment   None.

Playing Time   Several minutes per round.

Rules of Play   One player at a time acts the part of Beelzebub, your guide to the nether world. Beelzebub chooses a category of words, such as the names of fruit that begin with the letter "p" (persimmons, peaches, pomegranates, plums, pears, papaws, passion fruit, pineapples, etc.). Or, he can choose something less specific, such as names of objects in the room that are clearly visible to all players (chairs, lampshades, magazines, carpets, wristwatches, shoes, purses, and so on). He can also pick a rather subtle category, such as names of things that hang (paintings, drapes, earrings, neckties, pendants, rope ladders, and such).

Beelzebub gives the rest of the players one clue at a time in the form of a word that fits his category. In the first example above, Beelzebub might start things off by saying, "I'm bound for hell and I'm taking *persimmons*. What are you taking?" and then wait for responses from the group. A player who thinks he has a word that will also fit the category asks Beelzebub in this manner: "If I bring *peaches*, can I come too?" Since the word fits, Beelzebub answers that yes, the player may go to hell, too. Otherwise, another player makes a guess. Beelzebub *must* be honest and not change the category during the game.

If the group is stumped or becomes impatient, Beelzebub should continue throwing out clues. Each round lasts until all players are bound for hell. The *first* player to name a word that is acceptable gets to act the part of Beelzebub for the next round of play.

Sample Game   In the following game, the secret category is words that begin with one of the five vowels.

Beelzebub: All right, friends, listen carefully. I'm bound for hell and I'm taking *alcohol*. What are you taking?

First Player: If I bring my *bourbon*, can I go too?

Beelzebub: No, you may not. Bourbon is not allowed. (Pause.) But here's another clue. I'm bound for hell and I'm taking all the *underwear* I can pack. Plenty of *undershirts*. Plenty of *undershorts*. Now, what'll you bring?

Second Player: *Socks*!

Beelzebub: Nope. No socks allowed.

First Player: If I bring *coveralls*, can I come too?

Beelzebub: No, I won't allow coveralls ... though I would have allowed *overalls*.

Third Player: Can I go if I bring *oranges*?

Beelzebub: Yes, you may go.

Second Player: *Apples*?

Beelzebub: Yes, you may go also.

First Player: Okay, I'll bring some *pears*.

Beelzebub: No, you won't. Pears are not allowed.

First Player: How about *lemons*?

Beelzebub: Nope.

First Player: I give up.

Beelzebub: Don't give up yet. Let me review what the rest of us are taking. We're bound for hell

and we're taking *alcohol*, *underwear*, *overalls*, *oranges*, and *apples*. I will also be taking *eggs*. Now, what will you bring?

First Player: Can I go if I bring the *ice*?

Beelzebub: Yes, you may go.

Variation BOUND FOR HELL WITH THE STARS

In this version, the categories are groups of well-known people rather than objects. For example, categories might be the names of celebrities who have played on the TV show *Hollywood Squares* (George Gobel, Joanne Worley, Wally Cox, Charlie Weaver, Paul Lynde, Rose Marie, for example), or the names of celebrities whose first and last names begin with the same letter (Suzanne Somers, Bert Bacharach, Melba Moore, Ronald Reagan, Howard Hughes, Alan Alda, Mitch Miller).

SIMILES

Goal   To figure out the other team's similes in less time than it takes them to figure out yours.

Number of Players   2 teams of any number.

Equipment   Paper, pencils, and a stopwatch.

Playing Time   About 30 minutes.

Rules of Play   Separate the two teams out of earshot and give each a pencil and a sheet of paper to write down similes. You know what a simile is, right? Sure as shootin'. (That's a simile.) Each list should contain as many similes as there are players on the other team. If you want to make the game last longer, use twice that many.

When both teams are finished making their lists, they select which team will go first. The teams sit facing each other, and the player on one end of the team going first stands up to start the game. The player opposite him on the other team holds the list and the stopwatch. Simultaneously, he reads a simile from the list and starts the watch running. The watch will run until the player standing has answered the simile correctly. For example, the player with the list says "Black as . . ." and the other player must try to fill in the simile. He must complete the simile exactly as the other team has written it. It might be "Black as night," or "Black as the ace of spades," or something else.

If a player takes a guess and is wrong, he must wait five seconds before he can try again. If he feels he cannot get the answer, he can sit down after at least one

guess, and the next player in line will stand up to re-place him. This next player must try to answer the same simile. He, too, has the option of sitting down after at least one guess. As soon as he gives the right answer, the watch stops, the next player stands up, and the opposing player starts the watch and reads another simile. Continue with the same team until all the similes have been answered, then write down the total elapsed time. Give the watch to the other team, which reads its list and times the second team's answers. The team with the lowest time wins.

Here are some examples of similes you can use:

Happy as . . . a lark, a pig in mud, a sleeping dog.
Hard as . . . granite, nails, old cider.
Thick as . . . thieves, a milkshake.
Smooth as . . . silk, satin, glass, a cloud, a Cadillac,
water off a duck's back.

NO-NO

Goal To keep a chain of rhyming words going as long as possible.

Number of Players 2 are enough, 6 or 7 are about perfect.

Equipment None.

Playing Time Up to 10 minutes per round for a group of good rhymers.

Rules of Play To begin, someone thinks of a word that will be easy to rhyme with other words, then "defines" it briefly. The definition is actually that of a rhyming word, not the word itself. The player to the left must take this jumbled definition and figure out the word the first player really meant to define. He announces the word the first player defined, and gives a definition of yet another word that rhymes with the first two. A player has one minute to figure out the word he is supposed to give and come up with a definition. If he can't think of it within the time limit, he drops out of the game. The one player left at the end is the winner. Here's an example of a game among five players:

Phil (beginning the game): A *chair* is an animal with four legs.

Chris: No, no, you mean *bear*, which you comb every day.

Tom: No, no, you mean *hair*, which is my favorite fruit.

Joan: No, no, you mean *pear*, which is like a cave.

John: No, no, you mean *lair*, which is a bad poker hand.

Phil: No, no, you mean *pair*, which hops around.

Chris: No, no, you mean *hare*, which is something you take.

Tom: No, no, you mean *dare*, which is what I'm doing to you now.

Joan: No, no, you mean *glare*, which neighs and whinnies.

John: No, no, you mean *mare*, which is a big job.

Phil: No, no, you mean *mayor*, which is what you are right now.

Chris: No, no, you mean *player*, as in sooth.

Tom: No, no, you mean *sayer*, like a hunter.

"Mayor" is a perversion of the rhyme scheme. Players must now come up with words that consist of two syllables instead of one. However, if no one objects to a stretch like this, the game can continue. When the majority of players feel that a new word does not rhyme at all with the previous word, the player suggesting it must drop out of the game.

No-No is perfect for a large party, since it can be played with any number of people, and players can sit anywhere as long as some order is established to pass the definitions along in a consistent direction. It is an ideal amusement for a long car ride.

WORD LOGIC

Goal   To uncover a hidden word through deduction.

Number of Players   2

Equipment   Paper and pencils.

Playing Time   About 10 minutes.

Rules of Play   *Word Logic* is based on an old game called *Jotto*, and is included here for this reason: Commercial games just like it sell on the market for up to $60. So, here is the same expensive game, without the beeping, blinking, and cost of an electronic machine.

One player writes down a five-letter word in which none of the letters are repeated. He must not let the other player see it. The other player then takes his first turn by guessing a five-letter word and writing it on another piece of paper. The first player looks at the guess and writes down next to it the number of correct letters — that is, the number of letters in the guess that

are in his hidden word. With this information, the second player makes another guess (he writes it just below the first word), and again the first player writes down the number of correct letters. Play continues in this manner until the second player guesses the word correctly.

Then the roles are reversed and the second player writes down a secret word for the first to guess. Whoever discovers the other's word in fewer guesses is the winner.

DIVINATION

Goal   To trick the other players.

Number of Players   Any number.

Equipment   None.

Playing Time   About 10 minutes.

Rules of Play   To accomplish this divining trick, two players work in cahoots. One player announces that his friend will perform a bit of magic, and sends him out of the room. While he is gone, the rest of the group decides on a word he is to divine. When they decide on one, they call the performer back into the room.

The performer figures out the word through clues

that the other player gives him. In fact, the partner actually spells out the word for him. He spells out the word in this manner: He refers to consonants by the first letter of any statement he makes or question he poses; for vowels, he taps his foot — once for "a," twice for "e," three times for "i," four times for "o," and five times for "u."

If the performer is good enough, he should have no trouble divining the word. See if you can figure out what these clues say: "Having a tough time?" . . . (tap once) . . . "May I give him a clue?" . . . "Shame on you!" . . . "Time's almost up" . . . (tap twice) . . . "Really, you should have it by now!"

Answer: HAMSTER

WORD SERIES

Goal   To discover your opponent's word, or to stump him with yours.

Number of Players   2.

Equipment   Paper and pencil.

Playing Time   About 2 minutes per round.

Rules of Play   The player who goes first writes down three consecutive letters from his word on a sheet of paper, leaving room on both sides to add more letters.

The object of the game is for the second player to guess the word the first player has in mind. After each incorrect guess, which counts as one point against the guesser, the first player must add one more letter at one end of the sequence. After a predetermined number of rounds, the player with the fewer number of points wins.

Here is an example of how the game is played. The word Will had in mind was "ANNIVERSARY."

Will: IVE
Phil: ARRIVE?
Will: IVER
Phil: UNIVERSE?
Will: NIVER
Phil: UNIVERSITY?
Will: NIVERS

Phil: CONNIVERS?
Will: NIVERSA
Phil: UNIVERSAL?
Will: NIVERSAR
Phil: ANNIVERSARY!
Will: Correct. Your score is six.

ACTION AND OUTDOOR GAMES

ISOLATION

Goal   To be the last player left with a leg to stand on.

Number of Players   2 to 6, plus a referee.

Equipment   A square-tiled floor or chalk and pavement.

Playing Time   10 minutes.

Outdoor

Rules of Play   This is a variation of the board game of the same name by Lakeside, and requires only two skills — strategy and balance. It is the only game of its kind. For two players, you need a four-by-eight grid of squares like the one shown, each square large enough to accommodate a player's foot. A square-tiled floor is a convenient playing board. Or, you can draw a board on the pavement with chalk.

Each player starts with his feet in the two center squares on the last rows as shown in the diagram. Your turn consists of taking a step to any empty square with one foot, "crossing out" the square that foot left, and also crossing out the empty square of your choice anywhere on the board. To cross out squares (this means they cannot be used again in the game), use chalk or lay an object on the square. The referee performs this task.

You lose when you cannot reach an empty square on your turn or when you lose your balance. After a few turns, the choices of where to move your foot become limited since your opponent will probably cross out squares near you with every turn. You must plan your moves wisely. Don't box yourself into a corner from

which you cannot reach an empty square on your next turn. You can stretch as far as you like as long as you touch neither your opponent nor any square but the one you reach for. If your opponent is blocking a square you wish to try for, you may ask him to freeze while you attempt to get there without touching him.

You always have the option of standing on one foot. If you begin your turn with both feet on squares, you may lift a foot without putting it back on another square. You would cross out the vacated square as well as any empty square of your choosing, then remain balanced on one leg until your next turn. Beginning your next turn with one foot in the air, you may either hop to another square or simply place the raised foot on an empty square. If you hop to another square, cross out the square you left plus a square of your choosing. If you use your turn to set your raised foot down on an empty square, you can only cross out the square of your choosing.

Enlarge the grid to suit the number of players. For three players, use a five-by-eight grid; for four players, an eight-by-eight grid; for five players, an eight-by-ten grid; for six players, an eight-by-twelve grid.

NON-EQUIPMENT BASEBALL

Goal   To score more runs than the other team.

Number of Players   16 to 24.

Equipment   A baseball field.

Playing Time   About 45 minutes to an hour.

Outdoor

Rules of Play   Sixteen to 24 players, divided into two equal teams, play on a baseball field with foul lines, base paths, an outfield fence or boundary, and bases, but no balls or bats. Defensive players position themselves anywhere on the playing field. Offensive players divide into two lineups: runners and "balls." The first runner starts at home plate and the first ball anywhere outside the foul line in right or left field. To start, the ball enters the playing field and the runner heads for first base. If the runner can reach first before the ball is tag-

ged or forced out of bounds by a defensive player, he is safe on first. As long as the ball remains untouched in the outfield, the runner may choose to continue on to second, third, and home. When the ball is tagged, the runner is out; defensive players must stop where they are and may not move from that position until the next ball (another offensive player) enters the field.

As soon as the ball is tagged and the runner is put out, another runner and ball take their turn. Play continues in this way until three runners have been called out (at which point offense and defense switch places). Any runner who has reached base safely may try to advance while another ball is free in the outfield, but the most advanced runner who is off base when the ball in play is tagged or forced out of bounds is out. If two or more runners are on the same base when the ball is tagged or goes out of bounds, all but the first runner to reach that base are out. This is the only case in which a double play can occur. A run is scored when a runner crosses home plate safely, and the team with the most runs after a fixed number of innings is the winner. In case of a tie, play extra innings. For an added thrill, play on a muddy field.

MULTI-SOLO SOCCER

Goal   To score goals against all opponents.

Number of Players   3 to 7.

Equipment   1 soccer ball and 2 stakes per player.

Playing Time   About 30 minutes.

Outdoor

Rules of Play   Each player has his own goal, which consists of two stakes stuck in the ground, two to three feet apart. These goals are all at an equal distance from a center point. If five were playing, the field would look like the illustration on page 34.

To begin play, everyone stands in his own goal. A soccer ball is placed on the center point and someone yells "Go!" The object is for each player to score points by kicking the ball through an opponent's goal. The ball must be on the ground when it goes through the goal. (This keeps players from taking wild shots.) The last person to touch the ball before it goes through a goal

makes a point and the person whose goal it goes through loses one (making negative scores possible). When a goal is scored, the ball remains in play. It is up to the players to decide if goals can be scored from both sides of a goal, or only through the side facing the center. Play is continuous. No territory is out of bounds.

Note   A high level of skill is not necessary for this game. A good ''goal poacher'' can often get a foot on someone else's shot and claim the point for himself. There's no rule that outlaws extensive goal guarding, but you'll never score that way. To make the game easier or more difficult, move the goal stakes farther apart or closer together.

DATA PROCESSING

Goal To order your team before the other.

Number of Players At least 4 people per team, plus a referee.

Equipment None.

Playing Time As long as you like.

Rules of Play Form two lines of equal length and face each other. At the signal "Go," each player states his first name and the two lines reorganize into alphabetical order. Next, everyone states his *last* name and the lines reorganize into a new alphabetical order. The processor (referee) continues "handling" data—

birthday, house or apartment number, street name, and so on. Scoring is based on time and accuracy, and can be varied to suit the mood of the group. In one version, the fastest team wins, provided it makes at least three fewer errors than the other team.

Variation For a small group, play with just one line and don't worry about scoring.

RATTLESNAKES

Goal To find and bite (tag) the other rattlesnake.

Number of Players 2 at a time.

Equipment 2 coffee cans and a handful of coins.

Playing Time About 10 minutes per round.

Outdoor

Rules of Play This game is best played with a large group of people outdoors. Choose two players to be the rattlesnakes and have the rest of the group form a circle around them about 15 feet in diameter. Blindfold the two rattlers and place them at opposite sides of the circle. Give each snake a coffee can with a few coins in the bottom to hold in one hand. Then, spin each snake around to get him disoriented as to where the other snake is.

On the signal "Go," the rattlesnakes begin wandering around the circle (being kept in bounds by the other players), trying to find and bite (tag) the other one. To get a fix on his opponent, a snake can shake his rattle (can). The other snake must respond immediately by shaking his. A snake may not shake his rattle more than three times without the other snake initiating a shake of his own. You may play that one bite kills a snake, or, to make the game last longer, that each snake can withstand three bites.

DRAGON'S TAIL

Goal   For the head of the dragon to catch its tail.

Number of Players   At least 6, more is better.

Equipment   None.

Playing Time   About 15 minutes.

Outdoor

Rules of Play   Form a dragon, or several dragons if you have enough players, by having people line up and put their hands around the waist of the player in front of

them. Now, the object is for the person at the front of the line (the dragon's head) to catch hold of the person at the end of the line (the dragon's tail) and circle his waist with his hands. The tail tries fiercely not to be caught. When he's caught, the old tail becomes the new head and the game begins again.

Play until everyone has had a chance to play both the head and the tail at least once. If you have more than one dragon, have them chase each other!

IDIOT'S DELIGHT

Goal   To aim and throw cards at targets.

Number of Players   2 or 4.

Equipment   A standard deck of playing cards and a sheet of newspaper.

Playing Time   About 10 minutes.

Rules of Play   Lay the paper on the floor, at least 10 feet from the players, with the sections labelled "3" and "4" closest to them. One player uses black cards and the other player uses red cards. Or, the players can use cards with different designs on them.

In the two-player game, the players alternately toss three cards each, trying to land them on the newspaper. As in shuffleboard, a card may dislodge another from the board or to another square. When the two players have each thrown their three cards, they tabulate the

score, giving themselves the point value of the section of the newspaper on which their cards have landed. Thus, a card that has landed on the section labelled "3" earns three points, and so on. Each player takes 10 turns, and the player with the highest final score wins.

The four-player game is a team effort, two players against two. But in this variation, players only throw two cards each. Again, play 10 rounds.

PRUI

Goal   To find the Prui and become part of it.

Number of Players   A large group, plus a referee.

Equipment   None.

Playing Time   About 10 minutes.

Rules of Play   After establishing some rough boundary lines, the players close their eyes and begin to wander around looking for the Prui. The referee whispers into one player's ear that he is the Prui, and that player opens his eyes. Whenever a player bumps into another, he shakes hands and asks, "Prui?" If the answer is "Prui?" he knows he hasn't found it. If there is no re-

sponse, he again asks, "Prui?" If again no response, he knows he's found the Prui. He may now open his eyes, hold hands with the Prui, and become part of it himself. Now, when other players ask "Prui?" he must not respond. They join him in the Prui.

The object is for all players to eventually be connected by holding hands. When a player bumps into clasped hands, he feels his way to the end player, asks "Prui?" and becomes part of it.

RUNNING THE NUMBERS

Goal   To be the first team to circle all of the numbers on its chart.

Number of Players   An even number per team, plus a referee.

Equipment   Pencils, slips of paper, 2 poster-size sheets of paper, 2 boxes or hats.

Playing Time   About 10 minutes.

Rules of Play   First, prepare two identical charts of numbers, in which the numbers are randomly arranged in a grid pattern as shown in the illustration. The charts can be complex or simple, but they must be identical. Next, on each of two sets of paper, write out 15 different numbers. Use the same numbers for each set. The numbers should have two, three, four, or five digits, depending on how difficult you want the game to be.

Choose two teams, each with the same number of players, and line them up about 10-feet apart, facing the

same direction. Place the charts far enough away so that no one from either team can read the numbers from where he is standing. Also, tilt the two charts away from each other so that when a player stands in front of one chart, he cannot read the other one. Put a set of numbers into each box (hats will do), and set the boxes near the players in the front of each line.

On the signal "Go," a player from each team draws a slip of paper from the hat, runs to his chart, finds the number on the chart (either vertically, horizontally, or even diagonally) and circles it with the pencil, drops the pencil, runs back to the starting line, and tags the next player, who is then free to draw a number and repeat the process. The first team to find and circle all its numbers wins.

Variation Try the game with two identical *Find-a-Word* puzzles from a newspaper or another publication.

STORKS

Goal   To cause your opponent to lose balance.

Number of Players   2 or more, plus a referee.

Equipment   As many water pistols as you have players.

Playing Time   5 minutes per round.

Outdoor

Rules of Play   For two players at a time, this game goes rather quickly. Have them stand on one foot about five feet apart, facing away from each other. Each stork holds his raised foot behind him in one hand and a water pistol in the other hand. Then, on the signal

"Go!" the storks go into battle, trying to maintain balance at all times because the first to let go of his raised foot loses the game. There are no boundaries or other rules to this game, so anything goes. Obviously, a squirt of water to the opponent's face is a good strategy. Just as obviously, the game should be played outdoors.

With a large group you can play a round-robin elimination tournament, pitting players against each other two at a time. Or you can pit several storks against each other in the same battle. To begin a game with many players, have them form a rough circle with all players facing away from the center.

KNOTS

Goal   To get your group tangled, then untangled.

Number of Players   6 to 15.

Equipment   None.

Playing Time   About 10 minutes.

Rules of Play   The players form a circle so that everyone is as close to the center as possible. The players close their eyes, then everyone reaches both arms straight into the center and blindly grabs two other hands. Now, opening their eyes, the players try to untangle themselves without breaking any of the hand connections unless absolutely necessary. Most of the

time this can be accomplished by shifting bodies through loops of arms, and such. One player can be the director and tell the other players who should move where, or everyone can just try to untangle themselves at once.

SIMON DOESN'T SAY

Goal   To be the last player eliminated by Simon.

Number of Players   At least 4.

Equipment   None.

Playing Time   10 or 20 minutes, depending on Simon's skill.

Rules of Play This game is played in the same way as the children's game of "Simon Says," but backwards! First, pick someone to play the part of Simon, and line the other players in front of him. Set a time limit (10 to 20 minutes), during which Simon must eliminate all players or else the remaining players win. Simon proceeds to give commands to the players, such as "Simon says take two steps forward," "Lift one foot and hop," or "Simon says lift one foot and hop." The idea is for players not to do a command that begins with "Simon says. . . ." Only when Simon gives a command without this introduction do players have to follow his instructions. A false start or wrong move eliminates a player from the game. That's all there is to it, but it sure is fun.

ANNIHILATION

Goal   To remove all your opponents from the playing area.

Number of Players   At least 4 per team, plus a referee.

Equipment   None.

Playing Time   About 15 minutes.

Outdoor

Rules of Play   Please enjoy this game in the spirit of the New Games Foundation: "Play hard, play fair, nobody hurt." This is *not* an indoor game. *Annihilation* should be played on grass, sand, or some other soft surface. Divide your group into two equal teams plus a referee (or two).

Mark off boundaries about 30 feet in diameter. The referee starts the two teams from opposite ends of the boundaries. To distinguish opposing players, one team wears socks and the other goes barefoot. All players begin on their knees, and they cannot rise up beyond a kneeling position. If they do, they are automatically out of the game. The object is to force all opponents completely out of bounds, using all methods short of brutality. A player in pain must be left alone immediately, though the penalty for crying wolf is expulsion. When a player has no part of his body left in bounds, he is out of the game. The first team to throw out all opposing members wins.

THE HUMAN ALPHABET

Goal   To spell letters of the alphabet with your bodies.

Number of Players   At least 6, but as many as you can get.

Equipment   None.

Playing Time   About 20 minutes.

Outdoor

Rules of Play   Although this is really a noncompetitive game, you will need two teams of roughly the same size, with at least three or four people per team.

Separate the teams by 50 to 100 yards, if possible, and have the first team begin by forming the letter "A" with any or all of the players' bodies so that the other team can recognize it. When the players on the second team decide the first has formed a decent "A," they should show their appreciation by applause. Then it is up to the second team to form a "B" to the satisfaction of the first team.

Play continues through the alphabet; then the teams can spell words if there are enough players. When the players on one team tire of another team's attempt to spell something, they should show disapproval by trying to form the same thing themselves.

HUNKER HAWSER

Goal   To cause your opponent to lose balance while maintaining yours.

Number of Players   2 at a time.

Equipment   A 15-foot piece of rope and 2 small pedestals.

Playing Time   Anywhere from 1 second to 1 hour, depending on the skill of the players.

Outdoor

Rules of Play   Set the two pedestals (milk crates, cinder blocks, logs, or whatever) about six feet apart and have the two players stand on them with both feet. The

players must "hunker down" onto their haunches, whereupon they are each handed an end of the rope. Coil the slack between them.

On the signal "Hunker!" the players haul in rope and a tug-of-war ensues. The first player to touch any part of his or her body to the ground loses. Also, letting go of the rope entirely disqualifies a player. Players must have some part of the rope in hand at all times.

Hint Learn to let the rope slide through your hands just as your opponent gives a good yank. He'll go over backwards in surprise.

BELLRINGER

Goal   To cause the other team's bell to ring while keeping yours from ringing.

Number of Players   At least 8, more is better.

Equipment   2 small metal bells.

Playing Time   About 10 minutes, but you can make this game last as long as you like.

Outdoor

Rules of Play   This game requires at least the space of a small backyard and should be played outside. The group chooses two team captains, who alternately choose up sides. Two goals, such as trees or bushes, are established at opposite ends of the playing field, and the teams group near these goals to begin the game.

Each team captain is given a small metal bell and a piece of string with which he must tie the bell around his waist or through a belt-loop so it dangles freely. The other members of each team serve as the captain's guards, and surround him in a protective circle. The object is to transfer the captain back and forth between the two goals without ringing the bell. Whenever a captain makes a trip from one goal to the other without ringing his bell, his team scores a point. Any noise from a bell sends that team captain back to the goal from which he just started.

Invariably during the game, some of the guards will want to become attackers, heading off to make the other team's bell ring. Players may use any method

short of hurting their opponents to get the bell to ring, as long as they don't touch the bell itself. However, they should not leave their captain totally unprotected in case of a counterattack by the other team.

There are two ways to end the game. One is by an agreed-upon time limit, at the end of which the team with the most points wins. The other way is to set a goal limit (say, five goals), in which case the team to reach the set number of goals first wins.

POPULATION EXPLOSION

Goal   To fit as many people as you can on a small area rug without anyone touching the floor.

Number of Players   At least 8 or 10.

Equipment   A small area rug.

Playing Time   About 10 minutes.

Rules of Play   Place a small area rug on the floor. Players get onto the rug in such a way that no parts of their bodies touch the bare floor. If everyone stands on one foot and holds onto other players, as many as 20 people should fit on a bathroom rug.

THE LAP GAME

Goal   To seat everyone in a circle without chairs.

Number of Players   As many as you can get!

Equipment   None.

Playing Time   A good group can accomplish the task in
seconds.

Outdoor

Rules of Play   Arrange your group in a circle on the
lawn (or some soft surface) so that each player faces
another player's back at about half an arm's distance or
less. Instruct each player to hold his hands beneath the

elbows of the person in front. Then, in a rhythm the group can follow, announce, "One, Two, Three, Sit!" Everyone sits back onto the lap of the player behind. Often, someone goes off balance and the domino theory takes over. But when you succeed in seating all players comfortably, you'll be amazed at your perpetual human chair. According to the *Guinness Book of World Records*, the record for the human chair was set by 5,147 Girl Guides in Sydney, Australia, October 8, 1977.

Courageous groups have been known to go the *Lap Game* one better. When they've accomplished a successful seating, they perform a variation known as "Stand, Turn, Sit!" You can figure out what that means — and how hard it is to do!

HEADS VERSUS STOMACHS

Goal To build a chain of bodies without laughing.

Number of Players At least 5 and as many as possible.

Equipment None.

Playing Time About 10 minutes.

Rules of Play One at a time, players lie flat on their backs, with their heads placed on the next player's stomach as shown in the illustration. The chain can wind and turn all over the place, but both ends must

meet. The last player to lie down should be in a position to support the first player's head with his stomach.

The object of the game is to complete the chain using all players and connecting the ends into a circle without so much as a giggle from any player. If there is so much as a giggle, everyone is in a lot of trouble. The laughter will build up, transferring through stomachs from one player to the next until everyone is rolling on the floor. Never attempt *Heads Versus Stomachs* immediately after dinner.

ANARCHY

Goal To break through the grasp of the 2 players opposite you.

Number of Players 3 or more, always with an odd number.

Equipment None.

Playing Time A few minutes per round.

Outdoor

Rules of Play Gather your odd-numbered group of players into a circle with their backs facing the center and have them join hands firmly. You might want to alternate male and female players. The object for each player is to break the grasp of the hands of the two

players directly opposite him in the circle. For example, in the illustration, A has to break the bond between D and C, B has to break the bond between E and D, and so on. This is not as easy as it sounds, because players will be facing away from their targets and must attempt to break through with their backs and elbows, or by sitting on the players' hands. The winner is the first player to break through, and the two players who get broken apart are the losers. There are no rules governing play — anything goes in *Anarchy*. You are only limited by your conscience.

SPOONFULS

Goal To be the first team to fill your glass with water.

Number of Players At least 3 per team, more is better.

Equipment 2 tablespoons, 2 drinking glasses, and 2 pans of water.

Playing Time About 5 or 10 minutes per round.

Outdoor

Rules of Play *Spoonfuls* is a simple relay-race game to be played outside (unless you don't mind water being spilled all over your house). Choose two or more teams of equal number, and line up each one next to a pan of

water and a tablespoon. Place the water glasses about 15 feet from the starting lines. Then, on the signal "Go," the first member of each team grabs a spoon, scoops up a spoonful of water from the pan, and walks, runs, or crawls to his team's glass, deposits the water in the glass, runs back to the line, hands the spoon to the next player, and goes to the back of the line. It will probably take many turns to fill a glass with water. The first team to fill its glass wins. For a shorter race, use either larger spoons or smaller glasses.

UNITED NATIONS

Goal   To be the first team to find all of its "blind" countrymen.

Number of Players   At least 12, plus a referee; a larger
group is better.

Equipment   Paper, pencil, and blindfolds for all players.

Playing Time   5 or 10 minutes.

Rules of Play   The referee randomly hands each player
a slip of paper on which the name of a foreign language
has been written (Latin, Greek, German, and Russian
usually work well). He then blindfolds the players. The
referee must assign a language to roughly the same

number of players so that no team has the advantage. At the signal "Go," all players attempt to speak in their assigned native tongues as best they can, and group themselves with the players who sound as if they were their countrymen. The first team to thus group itself wins. Proper names and English words cannot be used. It is best to play this game at the beginning of the party as an ice-breaker.

GIANT PICK-UP STICKS

Goal   The same as in regular *Pick-Up Sticks*: To get all of your sticks out without disturbing the rest of the pile.

Number of Players   Depends on the number of sticks, but 3 or 4 players are enough.

Equipment   Cardboard tubes, all of the same size, pre-painted various colors. (These tubes are usually 3 feet long.)

Playing Time   20 minutes.

Outdoor

Rules of Play   Collect as many cardboard tubes as you can and paint them different colors. There must be an equal number of each color. Jumble them up on the lawn as you would jumble regular Pick-Up Sticks. Each player chooses to be a certain color, and on his turn tries to get one of his color sticks out of the pile without

disturbing the positions of the other sticks. He continues removing sticks until he disturbs the pile. Then play passes to the next player. The first player to get out all of his color wins.

UP AGAINST THE WALL

Goal   To be the first player to form a word of 4 letters or more.

Number of Players   A group of at least 8 or 10.

Equipment   Pencils, paper, and pins or tape.

Playing Time   Sometimes as much as 20 minutes.

Rules of Play   As each guest arrives, tape or pin to his or her back a piece of paper on which a letter of the alphabet has been written. Also give each guest a pencil and a piece of paper. Players slink around the room trying to see the letters on other players' backs without giving their own away too often. When a player sees a letter, he writes it down, along with the name of the guest on whose back he found it. (No fair withholding that information!) The first player to gather enough letters to form a word of four or more letters is the winner. Proper names are not allowed. Make sure the letters will not make it too difficult nor too easy for the guests to form words.

MEMORY GAMES

IMAGINE THAT!

Goal   To repeat more of the ever-lengthening sentence than any of your opponents.

Number of Players   2 or more (the more the merrier).

Equipment   None.

Playing Time   A few minutes per round.

Rules of Play   This wonderful party game is actually more of an exercise in group fantasy than anything else. Seat everyone, roughly in a circle, and choose who will start the game, after which play passes in a clockwise direction. The first player names an object that everyone can visualize. The second player must repeat it, adding some detail or description to the object. Then the third player repeats what he has heard and also adds something to it. And so on around the room as many times as you like. When it becomes a player's turn he must repeat the description correctly and add something to it, or drop out of the game. It is best to construct the image like a photograph or a still life. What you usually get is a wonderful little vignette, a sort of verbal snapshot in incredible detail. Here is an example of how the game is played:

First player: A rose.
Second player: A reddish rose.
Third player: A reddish rose in a vermillion vase.
Fourth player: A reddish rose in a vermillion vase on a fine oak table.

Fifth player: A reddish rose in a vermillion vase on a fine oak table for four.

Sixth player: A reddish rose in a vermillion vase on a fine oak table for four at a quiet bistro.

Seventh player: A reddish rose in a vermillion vase on a fine oak table for four at a quiet bistro overlooking the wide water.

Eighth player: A reddish rose in a vermillion vase on a fine oak table for four at a quiet bistro overlooking the wide water in the south of France.

Ninth player: A reddish rose in a vermillion vase on a fine oak table for four at a quiet bistro overlooking the wide water in the south of France facing a warm west wind.

You may end the game upon consent of all players when the image seems too perfect to expound upon.

Variation DO-RE-MI-FA

The same rules apply here, but players are trying to sing back an ever-lengthening melody of musical notes. The first player sings one of the four notes: do, re, mi, or fa. The next player sings it and adds one to it, and so on, until only one player is able to sing it. Memory counts. Quality of voice does not.

BLACK BOX

Goal To identify the most number of sounds from a tape recorder.

Number of Players 3 or more.

Equipment A tape recorder and prerecorded sounds.

Playing Time 30 minutes.

Rules of Play Someone must provide a tape recording of many everyday sounds: a soda can being opened, a quarter sliding into a vending machine, a refrigerator door closing, a fly being swatted, and so on. Each sound should be separated by about 10 seconds on the tape, and the entire tape should be played through without stopping. Players write down as many sounds as they hear. Depending on your audience, you may want to run the tape a second time. The player who identifies the most sounds correctly wins.

Variation BLACK SACK

One at a time, players reach into a sack (a pillowcase works well) filled with about 10 everyday items that are difficult to identify by touch alone.

Variation BLACK JAR

Players try to identify smells from jars or cans. Things that work well are asparagus, pencil shavings, pennies, and such.

THE TIBETAN MEMORY TRICK

Goal   To remember and repeat aloud as much of the tricky sentence as possible.

Number of Players   Any number, 1 at a time, with 1 person to read.

Equipment   This book.

Playing Time   No more than 5 minutes per player.

Rules of Play   One person, perhaps the host, is chosen to be the reader and another player volunteers to go first. The reader recites sentence one and the player repeats it. Easy enough. But then the reader reads sentence two, which adds something to sentence one. Still easy. Most players, however, find that it gets difficult by about sentence five or six. The slightest slip-up or pause and the player is replaced by another, who begins with sentence one. Play as many rounds as you like, keeping track of how far each player gets each time around the room. The player who gets the farthest wins. It takes years of play before most people tire of this game.

Here are the sentences.

1   One hen.
2   One hen, two ducks.
3   One hen, two ducks, three squawking geese.
4   One hen, two ducks, three squawking geese, four Limerick oysters.
5   . . . five corpulent porpoises.

6   . . . six pairs of Revlon tweezers.

7   . . . 7,000 Macedonians in full battle array.

8   . . . eight brass monkeys from the ancient sacred crypts of Egypt.

9   . . . nine apathetic sympathetic diabetic old men on roller skates with a marked propensity towards procrastination and sloth.

10   . . . 10 lyrical spherical diabolical denizens of the deep who stalk about the corners of a cove all at the same time.

When you master these sentences, or tire of trying, make up your own.

INGREDIENTS

Goal   To be the first team to guess the most foods.

Number of Players   At least 6.

Equipment   Paper and pencils.

Playing Time   About 30 minutes.

Rules of Play   Divide the players into two teams. One at a time, each team spends exactly five minutes in the kitchen looking at the canned, boxed, and bottled foods in the cupboards. Players select five foods and write the ingredients on a piece of paper. They do not write the names of the foods.

When both teams have returned to the living room (or wherever they play), they exchange their lists. Then, each team writes the names of the foods next to the descriptions of the ingredients. Even if players aren't sure of what a food is, they should guess. Players have 10 minutes in which to name the foods. The team that correctly names the most foods within that time wins. If neither team finishes before then, the team with the most correct answers wins. The team finishing first before the 10 minutes are up wins, provided it has more correct answers than the other team. Settle any disputes in the kitchen.

SPELL AND RUN BASEBALL

Goal   To score more runs than the opposing team by spelling words correctly.

Number of Players   At least 6 per team.

Equipment   Paper, pencil, and coins.

Playing Time   About 30 minutes.

Rules of Play   Draw a baseball diamond on a large piece of paper. Divide the group into two equal teams. Decide which team will go first (the Visitors) and which team will pitch first (the Home Team). The teams go to opposite ends of the house and write down as many words as they can think of that are hard to spell. Proper nouns and unfamiliar technical terms are not allowed. When each group has a list of about 50 words, they return to the play area.

One at a time, the Visitors stand up to bat. A player from the opposite team (the pitcher) reads the batter a word from his list and the batter must try to spell it immediately. If he spells it incorrectly, he sits down and it counts as one out against his team. If he spells the word correctly, he advances a token (coin) to first base and decides if he wants to try to steal second. If he elects to steal second base, the pitcher gives him another word. An incorrect spelling would again mean one out for his team, and a correct spelling would advance his token to second base. A run is driven across the plate only when the bases are full and the batter

gets a hit (spells a word correctly). A runner may never
try to steal a base that is already occupied.

After three outs, the fielding and batting teams exchange places. Play as many innings as you want. The
team with the most runs, of course, wins.

BORDERLINES

Goal To know your geography better than your opponents.

Number of Players At least 3 or 4.

Equipment A map atlas.

Playing Time About 20 minutes.

Rules of Play Play the first round of *Borderlines* with a map of the United States. Have all players, one at a time, study the map for 30 seconds. With a large group, let the players study the map in groups.

Once everyone has had a chance to study the map, elect one player to be the map reader. The map reader picks out a state at random and calls out its name. The

other players race to figure out how many states border on it, as well as what they are. Whoever comes up with an answer first blurts it out. If a player names an incorrect number of states bordering it, he must wait until another player tries an answer before he can go again. A player who correctly identifies the number of states receives five points. If that same player would like to go on, he may try to name the states bordering the state in question, receiving one point for every correct answer and minus three points for every incorrect answer. Or, he can leave the naming of individual states up to the other players.

After the map reader has called out and scored for five states, add up the points for each player and announce the winner. Then try a map of Africa!

SCHIZOPHRENIA

Goal   To guess combinations of famous people in photographs.

Number of Players   A group of 6 or more.

Equipment   Photographs cut from magazines and newspapers.

Playing Time   About 15 minutes.

Rules of Play   For this game, you have to do a little preparation. First, gather some old newspapers and magazines and look for photographs of well-known people. Cut them out and make composite photographs, using parts from different people to make up one head.

There should be some connection between the people in the photographs: Gene Kelly and Fred Astaire, Walter Cronkite and Barbara Walters, Sonny and Cher, Charlie's Angels, or perhaps the First Family.

Once you have at least half a dozen composite photos, you'll be ready for a good round of *Schizophrenia*. One player holds up the photos one at a time. The first player to identify all of the people in a photo gets a point. The player with the most points at the end wins. Or, you can just forget about the points and play for fun.

CARD,
NUMBER,
AND
STRATEGY
GAMES

HUMAN HINDU PYRAMID PUZZLE

Goal   To figure out the secret behind one of the world's oldest puzzles.

Number of Players   7.

Equipment   3 sheets of paper and a washable-ink marking pen.

Playing Time   5 to 30 minutes, depending on the ingenuity of your group.

Rules of Play   First, all seven players mark their hands with the washable-ink pen with a number from one to seven. Imagine that the hand marked "7" is the largest and the hand marked "1" is the smallest.

Once the hands are marked, lay three sheets of paper in a row on a table. The players stack their hands on the left-hand sheet in order from "7" on the bottom to "1" on the top. The object is now to transfer the hands to one of the other two sheets of paper, ending with them stacked in the same order in which they were stacked at the start of the game. To do this, players follow three major rules: 1) Move only one hand at a time; 2) Move only the top hand in any stack; and 3) Never place a larger hand on top of a smaller hand (that is, never cover a lower number with a higher number).

If you have fewer than seven people, several players can mark and use both hands. You'll need a minimum of four players to play this way. You can also try the puzzle solitaire. It's easy to make the pieces you need out of

paper or wood. If you want to start with an easier puzzle, use only five or six discs (hands). According to a legend behind the Tower of Brahma (which consisted of 64 stacked discs), monks transferring the discs at the rate of one per second would not finish their task of restacking the Tower of Brahma for trillions of years! Fortunately, your task can be accomplished here in 127 moves. See how close you can get.

DISPARAGE

Goal   To form words within a crossword grid.

Number of Players   2 to 6.

Equipment   Paper, pencils, and perhaps a dictionary to settle disputes.

Playing Time   About 20 minutes.

Rules of Play   Have each player draw a grid on a piece of paper. The five-by-five grid shown here is for two or three players; for four, five, or six players use a six-by-six grid; for a really large group, you can make an even larger grid.

Once each player has a grid, you can begin the game.

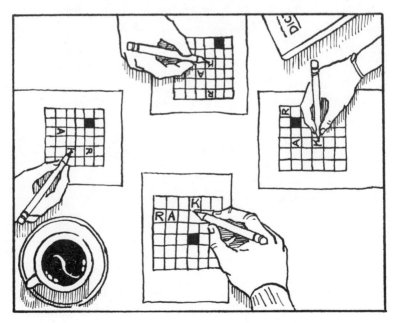

The first player calls out a letter in the alphabet. The other players write down that letter somewhere within their grids. The choice of where to place it is entirely up to each player. The object is to form words, crossword style (that is, words that read from left to right or top to bottom). Each player in turn (play proceeds clockwise) must call out a letter that the other players must use somewhere in their grids.

Players can call out a "blank" at any time during the game, which means the other players must darken in one square on their grids. However, you can only use four blanks during the game.

When the players have a full grid, they write down all of the legitimate words they can find. Remember, words must read from top to bottom or from left to right. Proper nouns and slang are not allowed, and a word may not be interrupted by a blank square. Score one point per letter for each valid word. A long word that contains a shorter word only scores once for the long word.

LIAR'S POKER

Goal   To win tricks, often by lying.

Number of Players   2 or more.

Equipment   10 1-dollar bills for each player.

Playing Time   About 20 minutes.

Rules of Play   If you don't want to gamble, make sure everyone gets back what he put in. Designate one player to be the dealer. The dealer starts the game by giving everyone 10 one-dollar bills, face-down. All players pick up the top bill in their stacks and study the eight-digit serial number, ignoring any letters that are part of it. The object of the game is to win each trick by bidding on how many times you think a certain digit occurs among *all* the serial numbers on the bills in play. Zero is the lowest digit, and nine the highest. The lowest bid that can be made is "One Zero," and the highest is "Eight Nines" (there are eight digits in serial numbers). Each player in turn must either raise the bid, challenge the bid, or pass, in which case he forfeits his dollar to whoever wins the hand. Study this example of a two-player game.

First Player (holding serial number 73869036): I bid two zeroes.
Second Player (holding serial number 05284981): I bid one one.
First Player (bluffing): Two ones.
Second Player (also bluffing): Two threes.
First Player (thinking the second player has two threes

in addition to his own two threes): I raise to four threes. Second Player (not believing the first player has four threes): I call your bid.

At this point, both players lay down their bills and count the total number of threes. Since the second player is right and there are only two threes, he wins the bills. If he were incorrect and there were at least the number of digits bid (if there were four threes), he would lose the bills. With more than two players, anyone can challenge a bid. Only the challenger or the challenged lose and win bills with each trick. Other players just place their bills at the bottom of their stacks.

As soon as one player has no more bills, he is out of the game. The last player left with bills is the winner.

LAST MOVE

Goal   To be the last player able to make a move.

Number of Players   2 to 5.

Equipment   Paper, pencil, and pennies (or other round objects).

Playing Time   About 5 minutes.

Rules of Play   The ancients played this game with stones and holes scooped out of the dirt. Here's another version. The number of players determines to some extent how many squares you wish to draw for a board. For two players, draw a line of 11 squares; for three, 15; for four, 19; and for five, 25. The line may curve, but

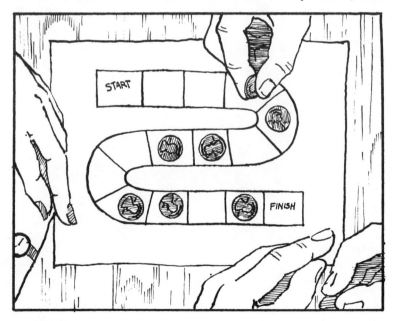

make sure each square is large enough so a penny (or whatever object you wish to use for stones) will fit inside it. Label one end "Start," and the other "Finish."

Once you draw the board, place a number of pennies randomly along the line so that there are more empty spaces than pennies, but close to half and half. Then, the first player picks up a penny and moves it to any open space in the direction of the "Finish," jumping over other pennies in the way. He may move it one space or many, so long as he places it on an empty space. The penny nearest "Finish" may never be moved. Play proceeds in this manner until no more moves can be made. The last player to have made a move wins.

Make your own variations of this game. For example, try playing without jumping over other pennies.

ARITHMETICAL CROQUET

Goal To be first to get to the "winning-peg."

Number of Players 2.

Equipment Paper and pencils.

Playing Time 5 minutes.

Rules of Play 1) The first player names a number not greater than 8. The second does the same. The first player then names a number that is higher, but no more than 8 digits higher, than his last number. Players alternate turns until one of them names 100, which is "winning-peg," and wins the game.

2) Ten, 20, 30, and the other multiples of 10 are the "hoops." To "take" a hoop, it is necessary to go from a number below it to one the same distance above it. To go from 17 to 23 would "take" the hoop 20, but to go to any other number above 20 would "miss it," in which case the player would have to go back to a number below 20, in his next turn, in order to "take" it properly. To miss a hoop twice loses the game.

3) It is also lawful to "take" a hoop by playing *into* it, in one turn, and out of it to the same distance above it in the next turn. To play from 17 to 20, and then from 20 to 23 in the next turn, would "take" the hoop 20.

4) Whatever step one player takes bars the other (on his next turn) from taking an equal step, or the difference between it and 9. If one player advances 2, the other may not advance 2 or 7. However, this rule does not apply when a player is playing *into* a hoop, or when he is playing from any number between 90 and 100 —

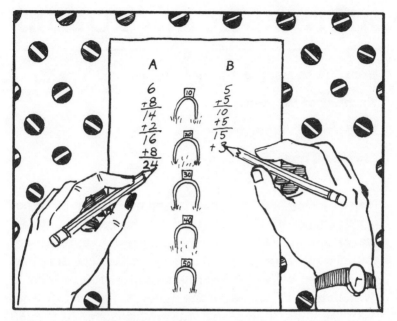

unless the other player is also at such a number, in which case the barring rule applies.

5) A player may miss the "winning-peg" once, but if he misses it twice, he loses the game.

6) When one player is "in" a hoop, the other player can keep him in by playing the number he needs for coming out. He can also do it by playing the difference between the number needed to come out and 9. He may go on playing the two barring numbers alternately, but he may not play either twice running. For example, if one player has gone from 17 to 20, the other can keep him in by playing 3, 6, 3, 6, and so on.

Special Note This little-known gem of a game for two was invented by Lewis Carroll in 1872. The version printed here was found among his papers dated April 22, 1889.

NINUKI-RENJU

Goal   To line up 5 of your pieces in a row before your opponent does, or to capture 10 of your opponent's pieces.

Number of Players   2.

Equipment   Paper, pencil, and stones (or other round objects).

Playing Time   About 10 minutes.

Rules of Play   In *Ninuki-Renju*, you play on the intersections of lines. First, draw a grid of nine lines by nine lines (you can use a larger playing grid once you get used to the game).

Then players alternately place a stone of their color

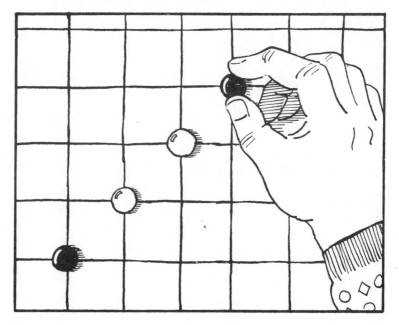

(heads or tails if they use pennies) on any open intersection on the board. No intersection may contain more
than one stone at a time. A player makes captures by
surrounding a pair of his opponent's stones with two
stones of his color. See the illustration, which shows the
placement of the second black stone that will enable
that player to remove the two white stones from the
board. The first player to capture 10 stones or to get five
of his stones in a row is the winner.

Special rule: A player may not place a stone where it
would single-handedly form two lines of open threes (an
open three is three stones in a row with no opposing
stones on either end). For example:

COMPULSION

Goal   To roll a good score with the dice.

Number of Players   Any number, plus a dealer.

Equipment   5 dice, poker chips or pennies, and pencil and paper.

Playing Time   About 20 minutes.

Rules of Play   Players sit around a table in a semicircle, facing the dealer. The dealer writes down the name of each player at the top of a sheet of paper according to this seating arrangement. Beneath each player's name, he will keep track of the betting and scoring. Give each player the same number of poker chips or pennies (about 15), and leave plenty for the dealer to pay off winning bets.

The dealer gives the five dice to the player on his left. This player starts the game by rolling all five dice onto the table. Depending on his strategy, the player then selects either the highest or the lowest die from this roll, and the dealer writes that number beneath the player's name. Next to this (in parentheses), the dealer records how many chips the player wants to bet on that turn. A player can bet any number, or none, of his chips. He then passes the dice to the next player. Play proceeds around the table in a clockwise direction. After all players have rolled once, the dealer removes one of the dice from play and hands the remaining four dice to the first player on his left. Again each player rolls the dice (four this time), selects one of them as his number, and places his bet with the dealer. At the end of this round, the dealer again removes one of the dice and starts another round with three, then two, and finally a single die. So, each player rolls five times and has a chance to place five bets.

The dealer now adds up the dice totals for each player. A score between 11 and 24 puts a player out of the game. If a player's five dice total 25 points or more, or less than 10, he wins chips from the dealer by rolling the five dice together to determine how much he is to be paid. Using the tables below, the dealer assigns him a Pay-Off Number. For each time that number comes up in his roll of the five dice, the dealer pays him the amount of his bet. So, if a player's Pay-Off Number is two, but he fails to roll any twos, he forfeits his bet. If he had rolled three twos, he would have received three times his bet.

Player's Total	Pay-Off Number
10	1
9	2
8	3
7	4
6	5
5	6
25	1
26	2
27	3
28	4
29	5
30	6

HERMIT'S CRIBBAGE

Goal   To score 121 points within 3 deals of the cards, according to standard rules of scoring *Cribbage*.

Number of Players   1.

Equipment   A standard deck of cards and a *Cribbage* board or pencil and paper to keep score.

Playing Time   About 10 minutes per successful game; 5 per unsuccessful one.

Rules of Play   After shuffling the cards, deal five face-down in a row. Turning over the rest of the cards one at a time from the top of the deck, place each beneath one of the five "cut" cards you have dealt face-down until you have four cards face-up for every cut card. Place the remaining cards to the side; you will not need them. (See the illustration.)

Turn over the five cut cards and score all five hands according to the rules of *Cribbage*. (Scoring rules for *Cribbage* appear at the end of this game.) Keep a running total of your score. You must reach 30 points on this first deal of the cards, otherwise you lose and must start over again. Assuming you reached 30 points with your first deal of five hands, shuffle all the cards and repeat the deal, scoring the five new hands as you did the first. On the second deal you must reach 60 points, otherwise you lose and have to start again. Assuming you reached 60 points on your second deal, you may shuffle the cards and deal out a third and final set of hands. On this deal you must reach 121 points to win the game.

For non-*Cribbage* players, this game is an excellent way to learn the scoring of the hands. If you're a *Cribbage* buff, this game will sharpen your skills and improve your strategic-planning ability. You should win every third game or so.

CRIBBAGE SCORING RULES   To count the score of a hand of four cards plus the cut card, form as many scoring combinations as possible out of the five cards. Here are the six different scoring combinations you can make.

1   You get two points for every combination of cards that totals 15. For example, the hand K of Clubs, Q of Diamonds, 5 of Diamonds, 3 of Clubs, and 2 of Hearts is worth eight points (two for the K+5, two for the K+3+2, two for the Q+5, and two for the Q+3+2; face cards are all counted as tens).

2   You get two points for every pair of cards you have. For example, the hand K of Clubs, K of Hearts, 7 of Spades, 7 of Hearts, and 3 of Clubs is worth four points (two for the kings and two for the sevens).

3   You get six points for three of a kind. For example, the hand K of Clubs, K of Spades, K of Diamonds, Q of Hearts, and 3 of Clubs is worth six points for the kings.

4   You get 12 points for having four of a kind. For example, the hand K of Clubs, K of Spades, K of Diamonds, K of Hearts, and 3 of Clubs is worth 12 points.

5   You get one point for every card that is part of a numerical sequence of at least three cards, regardless of suit. For example, the hand 10 of Spades, 9 of Hearts, 9 of Diamonds, 8 of Clubs, and 3 of Clubs is worth eight points (three for the run 10S-9H-8C, three for 10S-9D-8C, and two for the pair of 9s).

6   You get four points if all four cards in hand are of the same suit, and an extra point if the cut card is also of the same suit.

Special Rule   If a hand contains the Jack of same suit as the cut card, you get one point for "His Nob."

PASS IT ON

Goal   To go out with the highest pair of cards.

Number of Players   5 or more.

Equipment   A standard deck of playing cards.

Playing Time   About 10 minutes.

Rules of Play   Use twice as many cards as you have players. All but two of the cards should be pairs. In a five-player game, for example, select two aces, two twos, two threes, and two fours, ending with the mismatched pair of a king and queen. With three players, use two aces, two twos, and a king and queen. This will allow every player but one to eventually gather a pair of

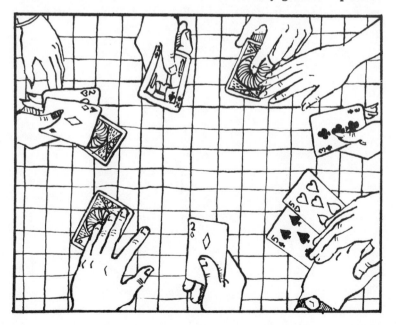

cards and go out. The idea is to avoid being stuck with the mismatched cards by passing them off on your neighbor.

Shuffle the cards and deal two face-down to each player. Play begins with anyone and continues as all players pass and pick up cards simultaneously. If a player starts the game with a pair, he has the option of laying his cards face-up on the table and announcing, "I'm out." If he doesn't have a pair, or if he has a pair and wants to stay in the game, he lays one of his cards face-down on the table in front of the player on his left. That player can either pick the card up to make his pair or pass it to the next player to his left. At no time does a player have to discard or pick up a card; however, a player can only pick up a card if he has just one card in his hand.

Since you'll probably play more than one round, use a point system for scoring: A pair of fives scores five points, a pair of aces scores one.

TURKISH CHECKERS

Goal   To capture all of the opponent's pieces.

Number of Players   2.

Equipment   A checkerboard and 16 checkers for each player (coins will do).

Playing Time   About 20 minutes.

Rules of Play   Set up the board as shown in the illustration. Players alternate turns. A turn consists of moving one checker one space straight forward or sideways or making a capture. Players make a capture by jumping over an opposing checker—again, either straight forward or sideways—to an open space directly on the other side, and then removing the captured piece from the board. As in American checkers, players can make a series of jumps over many pieces in one turn, using any combination of forward and sideways moves, capturing all pieces jumped. A player must always capture the greatest number of opposing checkers available to him.

Pieces may never move backwards. However, as soon as a piece lands on the back rank, it is crowned a King with another checker. Kings can move any number of spaces straight forward, backward, or sideways. A king makes a capture by jumping an opposing piece in one of those directions. It can jump from many squares away and need not land on the square directly beyond the piece being captured (which is removed immediately). When one player loses all of his men or is blocked from moving, he loses the game.

FORCED OUT

Goal   To *not* be the player forced to say "100."

Number of Players   2 or more.

Equipment   None.

Playing Time   About 15 minutes.

Rules of Play   Arrange your group in a circle and decide who will start the game. The first player names any number from 1 through 10. The next player adds a number from 1 through 10 to the first number and says that total. The third player adds a number to this total, and so on around the room in a clockwise direction.

The highest number a player can name is 100. When a

player has no choice but to say "100," he is out of the game. Then the next player begins a new round which continues until another player says "100" and is forced out of the game. Eventually one player will be left and he is the winner.

INDEX

Games for 2

Games for Groups of 6 or More

GAME CREDITS

"Anarchy" by A. Robison, "Non-Equipment Baseball" by Stephen Sniderman, "Multi-Solo Soccer" by Jonathan Maier," "Data Processing" by Jeffrey Fleece, and "Arithmetical Croquet" by Lewis Carroll are all reprinted from *Games* magazine (515 Madison Avenue, N.Y., N.Y. 10022). Copyright 1979 by Playboy.

"The Lap Game," "Hunker Hawser," "Rattlesnakes," "Knots," "Dragon's Tail," "Annihilation" by Stewart Brand, and "Prui" by Bernie DeKoven were all learned through the New Games Foundation.

"Word Series" by Doug and Jan Heller, "Tonto" by Pat McCormick, and "Black Box" were suggested by the National Puzzler's League as some of their favorites.

The rest of the games belong to you and me. They are ours because they have been handed down by the generation before us and because we will hand them down to the next generation. Thanks to all the game players who really created this book.